Farm Animals

This book belongs to:

____

By Glorya Phillips

Dog

Cat

Rabbit

Horse

Pony

Donkey

Cow

Bull

Buffalo

Goat

Pig

Sheep

Hamsters

Guinea Pig

Turkey

Cock

Hen

Goose

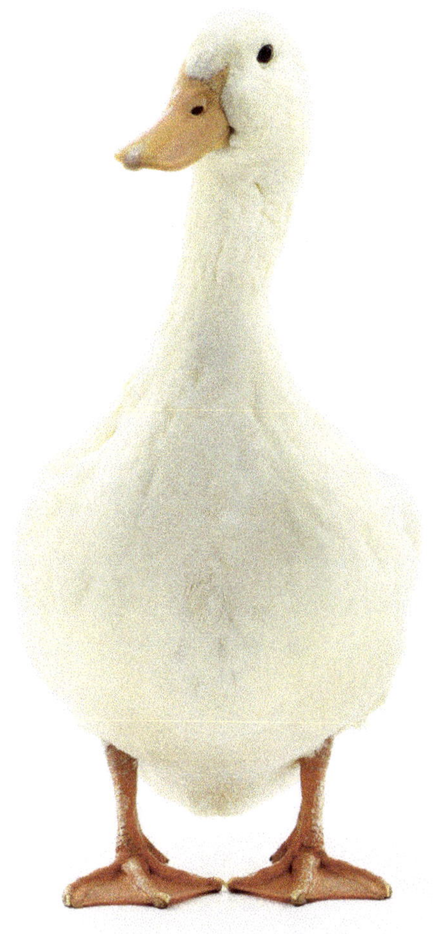

Duck

Guinea Fowl

Peacock

Parrot

Pigeon

Thank you for choosing us.

We hope you enjoyed our book.

Your feedback is important to us, please let us know how you like our book at:

 glorya.phillips@gmail.com

 www.facebook.com/glorya.phillips

 www.instagram.com/gloryaphillips